The Mad Monk Journeys from the Sea to the Temple

poems by

John Guzlowski

Finishing Line Press
Georgetown, Kentucky

The Mad Monk Journeys from the Sea to the Temple

Copyright © 2021 by John Guzlowski
ISBN 978-1-64662-525-3 First Edition
All rights reserved under International and Pan-American Copyright Conventions. No part of this book may be reproduced in any manner whatsoever without written permission from the publisher, except in the case of brief quotations embodied in critical articles and reviews.

ACKNOWLEDGMENTS

Five of these poems appeared in the Buddhist Poetry Review:
2
6
15
38
48

Thank you all for listening to these poems.

Publisher: Leah Huete de Maines
Editor: Christen Kincaid
Cover Art: Mieczyslaw Kasprzyk
Interior Art: Portrait of Ikkyū by Bokusai/public domain
Author Photo: Linda Calendrillo
Cover Design: Elizabeth Maines McCleavy

Order online: www.finishinglinepress.com
also available on amazon.com

Author inquiries and mail orders:
Finishing Line Press
PO Box 1626
Georgetown, Kentucky 40324
USA

Table of Contents

Ikkyū's Advice to a Traveler 1

The Sea 2

The Mountain Road to the Temple 7

The Village 19

The Temple 26

About the Author 33

Ikkyū was an eccentric, iconoclastic Japanese Zen Buddhist
monk and poet (1394-1481).
Sometimes he was considered mad, sometimes just funny.
He wrote poems about his life and the world around him
and the gods and spirits who travel through us.
The poems that follow here were not written by him,
were not imagined by him,
were not edited nor approved by him.
This is all my own doing.

Ikkyū's Advice to a Traveler

If you don't know
where you are going
you need to hurry up.

If you know
where you are going
you need to slow down.

The Sea

1.
The Monk Ikkyū
steps out of the water.

He knows an old man
comes out of the ocean
just the same way
a young man does,
wet and free.

Up the shore
the boats of the fishermen
wait for morning light
so they can leave.

2.
Ikkyū stands
at the edge
of the great sea.

He hears laughter.

It is the sound
of the sea blessing
the shore.

There are waves
in his eyes
so he shuts them.

3.
The Monk Ikkyū draws
on the shore

It is a poem
for the water

He knows the water
can't read
but he knows
it can dream.

4.
Here is the poem
he drew:

The earth yearns
for its sky
the way the wind
yearns for the sea
yearns to feel
its wetness
in its dryness.

5.
Ikkyū knows
every stream longs
for the sea
and that when we die
the water in the stream
will bring us home.

6.
If Ikkyū falls asleep,
his dreams don't.

They live
in the high, river country
of trees and sunshine.

7.
Darkness washes the beach.

Behind the clouds
the moon is a circle
drifting west.

Ikkyū stands on the sand
with his friends
looking at the sea
and at the moon.

They say nothing
just stare and wait
for the sea and the moon
to speak.

8.
Ikkyū sits on the pebbles
on the shore.

Nearby a fisherman
pulls in a net
heavy and sparkling
with fish.

Their tails beat
against the wind and the water
but still they go nowhere.

Ikkyū lifts some pebbles
with his hand.
The waves
have made them smooth.

Each feels to Ikkyū
like a beautiful bowl
but still he can feel
them rubbing his bottom.

Ikkyū knows
it's time to leave.

The Mountain Road to the Temple

9.
The forest road is hard,
the sun slanting down.

In a misty village above him
Ikkyū sees a crow land
on a frosted tree.

The fog is so thick
even birds can't caw
or sing through it.

Ikkyū knows he won't arrive
before snowfall,
but that's okay.

Once he's had
three warm cups,
he'll feel at home.

10.
Ikkyū waits on the forest path
for something to move,
a deer, a tree leaf,
a sparrow

But nothing moves,
nothing except the wind
and it doesn't speak to him
no matter how hard
he listens.

Ikkyū picks up his bundle
and walks deeper
into the forest.

11.
A farmer walks up
the ice-covered road
with a burden of straw
on his back.

He stops and asks Ikkyū
Why is there winter?

Ikkyū laughs and says
God gives earth winter
to show us the bones
of this place.

The farmer shakes his head
and turns back
to the road.

12.
Ikkyū studies the shadows
on the forest road
to the temple.

He knows they wait
like us for the bones
that will give them
breath and hope,
turn a leaf into a bird
a tree into the sky
on the road
to the temple.

13.
Ikkyū picks a leaf
from the ground
beneath the tree.

The leaf is dry,
cracked and bitten,
his brother.

He lets it fall
and it drops slowly
to the ground.

14.
In the night forest
Ikkyū dances before the campfire
with an old woman in rags.

She laughs and hides
her broken teeth
with a smile.

He starts singing
a song about sparrows
and holds her hand tighter.

Their dancing shadows
burn the darkness away.

15.
Ikkyū watches
the snow fall
at night.

He's happy it's warm
and that others
sleep in the shadows
with him.

16.
Ikkyū rises from the ground
and admires the shit
he leaves behind him.

He has heard some say
the world is full of shit
and that life is the shit
we must learn
to walk away from.

But oh,
the joy of shitting.

17.
Ikkyū remembers
when he was young.

Every old man
reminded him
of his father.

And now he knows
every man
is his father.

18.
Ikkyū wakes
from a dream.

He tries to remember
the look his mother
gave him
her smile
as he recited the poem
he wrote for her
but he can't remember.

There's only the darkness
and the words
of the poem

broken lines
broken words.

19.
Ikkyū waits to melt into snow
but the sparrow in his hands
sings a song that says
such dreams are foolish.

Better to smile
and sing with it.
He does.

20.
Ikkyū stands alone
before the forest.

It's dark
but that doesn't
frighten him.

Everything is dark at night
and it's always night.

21.
Ikkyū knows
this place.

It is always
this place
and not this place.

And every place
is never
and always home.

But still
every flower ends
in a dream.

22.
In the darkness
Ikkyū knows
he is lost.

If he knew the way
through the forest
he would go home.

If he knew the prayers
that would help him find it
he would say them.

But he doesn't
and so he asks the night
to hold him.

24.
Night waits beyond the hill
but Ikkyū still opens his book.

He knows in it he'll find
the silence and wisdom
and love he needs.

But after a moment
he looks at the words
in his hands.

They seem hard and wet
like rice that hasn't cooked
long enough.

He throws them
into a pot and waits
for them to boil.

25.
Walking, Ikkyū
finds three coins
on the forest road.

His purse is empty
so he leaves it there
with the coins.

26.
Hungry and walking,
Ikkyū lets the rain visit,
wash his face and hands.

It never stays long enough.

He wonders where it goes
when it's not here.

27.
Lonely and walking,
Ikkyū stares at the sky
and knows each prayer
in his hands is an orphan
and a sparrow.

28.
Dreaming and walking,
Ikkyū considers horses.

He knows they
can only run so fast
while a man can dream
more than he can dream.

29.
At night along the forest road
Ikkyū sits near the fire

and tries to remember the wisdom
his first master taught him,

but it was so long ago
and the master so drunk.

30.
Ikkyū loves night in the forest
the trees dreaming of the sky
and the sky dreaming of the water.

He loves to lie down near the campfire
and sleep the dream of dreaming.

He knows in the morning
there will be light in the dawn,
joys in the songs he sings,
hope in his grief and sorrow.

He will wake remembering
all the things he loves:
carrots and fresh bread,
the grayness of winter,
waking in his mother's arms.

31.
A peasant stops Ikkyū
on the road to the village
and asks for a prayer
or a word of advice.

Ikkyū pulls a prayer book
from his pocket
and says,

"Buddha is the light
that shadows us in its darkness
and teaches us that nonsense
is the wonder we all seek."

The farmer walks away
laughing.

32.
Standing
in the gray and white
winter forest
Ikkyū hears
a red bird sing.

Once there was
another bird
and they sang
a sweet song together.

Ikkyū knows
behind the trees
spring is waiting.

There is beauty
in every fallen leaf.

33.
Sitting by the fire
Ikkyū listens to the wind
and hears the voices
of the dead.

They talk about
the same things
the living talk about:

the day after tomorrow
and the rice in their bowls.

34.
Ikkyū watches
the darkness
beyond the circle
of fire in the camp

He knows night
wants to stay,
wants to dig its feet in
and hold on tight,
wants to see the sun
dancing like a tree.

But dawn will soon
be here

And then
where will darkness be?

35.
Ikkyū tells the forest
a story about his mother
and the way she cooked
rice and chestnuts.

The forest listens
and grows hungry.

36.
Ikkyū dances
before the fire.

His old feet are clumsy
stiff and broken
and still he leaps
and leaps again.

He hopes he lives
to tell this tale.

37.
Ikkyū looks
at the cup
in his hand,
the water warm
from the fire.

His father loved
to drink his water this way
in the early morning,
even before the sun rose.

Ikkyū loved
his father

And he drinks
this water slowly.

The Village

38.
Ikkyū sits
in the marketplace
and tries to explain
everything.

Here's what he says
to a soldier:

A tree is
the palm of my hand
and the face
of all there is
in the universe
to wonder about.

It is the tree to heaven
and its roots start
in my heart and yours.

39
In the village
Ikkyū watches
the men and women pass.

Sometimes they walk slowly
and sometimes they walk quickly.

The ones who walk fast
look forward and see nothing.

The ones who walk slowly
look everywhere
and see everything.

Ikkyū feels there should be
a true lesson here
but he's too tired
from walking slowly

and quickly
to understand it.

40.
Ikkyū watches
a man steal
some bread from
the bag of a friend.

As a child
Ikkyū stole all the time.
but never from friends.

They were like him.

So poor
even Buddha
would have looked
the other way.

Ikkyū looks
the other way.

41.
Ikkyū watches
an old man dance.

He's broken and bent
and dances in the dawn
between two houses.

He steps from their grayness
and becomes—for a moment—
a child of sunlight & yearning.

Ikkyū knows
there's no sorrow
greater than this,
no joy greater than this either.

42.
Ikkyū stands in a garden
among ferns growing
like soft and loving fingers.

He wonders
What is heaven?
What is hell?
Is this heaven?
Is this hell?

He finds a shady spot
and sits.

43.
Ikkyū plays
with a sword.

He flicks it slowly
watches the light
from the dawn sun
come and go
on the blade.

The sword's weight
is too much.

He puts it down
and enters his friend's house
to have breakfast.

44.
He opens the window.
The sun comes in
like a stranger
looking at him
and the room
wondering where
she could sit.

Anywhere, Ikkyū says.

45.
In a merchant's home
Ikkyū finally
comes to see
The truth of chairs.

Sitting in them
brings you pleasure
but it does not
bring you love.

46.
Ikkyū knows this village
is like every village.

Even when he's lost
standing on a crossroad
there are some people
who will help him.

47.
Ikkyū stands in a hut
listening to the sound of death
in an old woman's breathing.

Her breath is the sea
the message of its waves
on the shore—
their soft rush of foam
upon the sand.

In the corner
next to a candle
her son weeps.

48.
Ikkyū eats
a black cherry
and remembers
a dead friend

how much he loved
strawberries
their dark
sweetness
early in the morning.

The harvest
never lasted
long enough.

49.
Ikkyū stands
outside the dead woman's
bamboo hut.

In the dark and dry frost,
he stares at the stars.

They yearn
for his mouth
like honey.

The Temple

50.
Ikkyū enter the dark temple,
sees a monk sitting cross legged
in his robes
a lantern besides him.

The monk is lost in prayer
his eyes closed
his face stone.

Ikkyū hears a voice.
Somewhere
a child is crying
perhaps.

It's late and the road has been long.
He wishes for morning.

It doesn't come.

51.
After praying in the temple
Ikkyū closes his eyes
and waits for silence
the emptiness of gloves
a warm room where voices
speak words no one hears
where every shadow
recognizes every other shadow
where every darkness
is a brother to darkness.

Waiting is the rice
Ikkyū hungers for.

Rain begins to fall.

52.
Ikkyū sees
the snow at night
falling everywhere.

He pulls his cloak
tight around his neck
and wonders about Buddha.

He knew so much
but still he could not
tell us why the snow falls
or why life is a dark road
where we grow old so fast
and learn so little.

53.
Ikkyū sits and listens
to the devil talk.

The devil says he dreams
he swims in a river he can't escape.
It's a river made from his own blood,
the blood of the devil, thick and dark
like acid to the tongue.

He says he's lonely too.
He has no friends.
He misses everyone
and everything.

Soon the devil starts weeping.

54.
Ikkyū looks up,
sees a hawk
flying far off
in the broken clouds.

Ikkyū puts his hand
on the devil's back
and knows he is
his brother.

55.
Ikkyū listens to the wind
in the night temple.

He hears the silence.

It is the wind from nowhere
going nowhere
doing nothing.

He raises his hand
to feel it on his palm.
his palm smiles.

56.
The statue of Buddha
in front of Ikkyū
sits in silence.

The temple
dark since dawn,
empty as heaven
empty as souls.

Buddha waits
in the snow
for more snow.

His hands are a sparrow
listening to his silence.

Ikkyū kneels and knows
the snow will come
if he waits.

57.
Ikkyū hears a bell
in the darkness.

He knows what his teachers
taught him when he was a boy,
that the ringing of every bell
has three parts.

First *Atari*—
The sound is born.

Then *Oshi*—
The sound
repeats its soft
reverberations.

Then *Okuri*—
The echoing
that ends
in echoing
silence.

And the teachers
also taught him
what all this means:

Atari is birth
Oshi is life
Okuri is death

The sound of the bell
is the brother
of silence,
the sister
of darkness.

Ikkyū listens
till he hears
no more.

58.
Ikkyū knows
that Buddha
is always real
always here
and always watching
and always powerless
to do more than watch.

59.
If Ikkyū had disciples
he would say to them:

"Do without achieving.
Live like every day
is Wednesday."

They would laugh
and he would too.

60.
The temple is empty
and the path from it
is narrow and sunless.

Ikkyū sits on the hill
and peels an orange.

Old, he listens in silence.
The wind from the forest
warms his face.

In the valley below him
a boy walks on a white trail
and a bird flies across the sky.

Ikkyū waits for spring.

John Guzlowski's poetry appears in *Garrison Keillor's Writer's Almanac, North American Review, Rattle, Ontario Review, Salon. Com,* and many other journals. His poems and personal essays about his Polish parents' experiences as slave laborers in Nazi Germany and refugees making a life for themselves in Chicago appear in his award-winning memoir *Echoes of Tattered Tongues* (Aquila Polonica Press). He is also a columnist for the *Dziennik Zwiazkowy* (the oldest Polish language daily in America) and the author of *Suitcase Charlie* and *Little Altar Boy*, noir mystery novels set in Chicago. His most recent novel is *Retreat—A Love Story,* about two German lovers separated by war.

www.ingramcontent.com/pod-product-compliance
Lightning Source LLC
LaVergne TN
LVHW041602070426
835507LV00011B/1258